PRAYING MANTIS

by William Anthony

GROSS LIFE CYCLES

Enslow PUBLISHING

Please visit our website, www.enslow.com. For a free color catalog of all our high-quality books, call toll free 1-800-398-2504 or fax 1-877-980-4454.

Cataloging-in-Publication Data

Names: Anthony, William.
Title: Praying mantis / William Anthony.
Description: New York : Enslow Publishing, 2022. | Series: Gross life cycles | Includes glossary and index.
Identifiers: ISBN 9781978526518 (pbk.) | ISBN 9781978526532 (library bound) |
ISBN 9781978526525 (6 pack) | ISBN 9781978526549 (ebook)
Subjects: LCSH: Praying mantis–Juvenile literature.
Classification: LCC QL505.9.M35 A68 2022 | DDC 595.7'27–dc23

This edition is published by arrangement with Booklife Publishing

Published in 2022 by
Enslow Publishing
29 E. 21st Street
New York, NY 10010

Written by: William Anthony
Edited by: Emilie Dufresne
Designer: Amy Li

Printed in the United States of America

CPSIA compliance information: Batch #CWENS22: For further information contact Enslow Publishing, New York, New York, at 1-800-398-2504.

PRAYING MANTIS

Page 4	What Is a Life Cycle?
Page 5	Gross Life Cycles
Page 6	What Is a Praying Mantis?
Page 8	Egg Froth
Page 10	Nymph Wars
Page 12	Waiting for a Mate
Page 14	Off with His Head
Page 16	Death Sentence
Page 18	A Gross Life
Page 22	Gross Life Cycle of a Praying Mantis
Page 23	Get Exploring!
Page 24	Glossary and Index

Words that look like **this** can be found in the glossary on page 24.

WHAT IS A LIFE CYCLE?

All animals, plants, and humans go through different stages of life as they grow and change. This is called a life cycle.

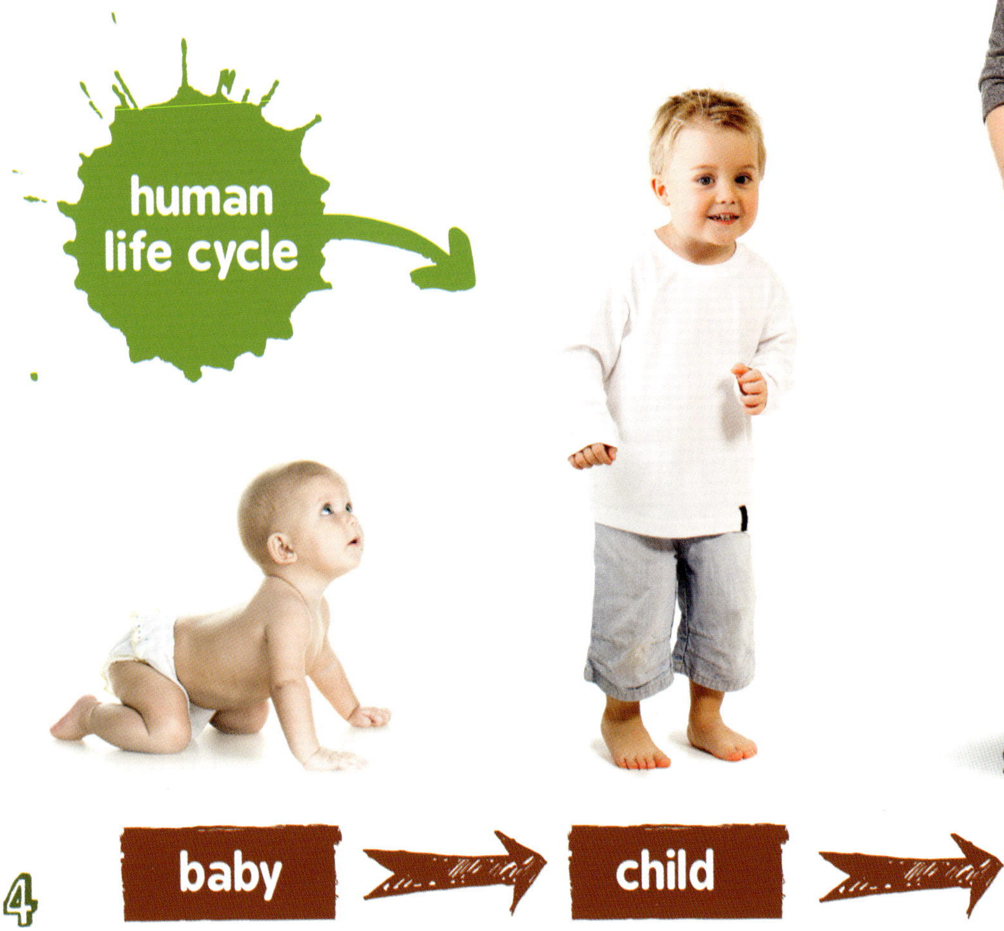

GROSS LIFE CYCLES

Not all life cycles are the same. They can be quick or slow. They can have lots of steps or very few. And some can be absolutely GROSS!

Life cycles can be stinky, smelly, and full of blood and guts. Gross!

WHAT IS A PRAYING MANTIS?

Praying mantises look like they are praying. This is how they got their name.

A praying mantis is a type of **insect**. Praying mantises have six legs. The back four legs are usually used for walking. The front two legs are usually used to catch **prey**.

Praying mantises have a terrifying, gross life cycle. There is a lot of chewing, chomping, and churning – and a terrible, scary end!

EGG FROTH

Praying mantises begin their lives as eggs. An adult female mantis may lay hundreds of eggs at one time. She lays them in an oozy froth.

Praying mantises usually lay their eggs before winter.

The froth quickly hardens around the eggs to form a hard case called an ootheca. The hard case **protects** the eggs from other animals and bad weather over the winter.

NYMPH WARS

Young praying mantises, called nymphs, will **hatch** from their eggs and leave the ootheca during the spring. When they leave, they are very hungry.

They are so hungry that they often end up eating their brothers and sisters! Full from their first meal, they set off into the world.

WAITING FOR A MATE

When the praying mantis has grown into an adult, it looks for a mate. Mates are two animals of the same kind that can make babies together.

Mating needs one female praying mantis and one male praying mantis. Many males find females by following **invisible** trails that females have left in the air.

OFF WITH HIS HEAD

Once the female mantis has mated with the male, she may do something terrifying. She may stop him from escaping and then bite his head off!

The female mantis may eat the male's head, followed by the rest of his body. Eating the male after mating helps the female make a lot more eggs than she normally would.

Some males escape and mate again, but many meet a painful end.

DEATH SENTENCE

The life cycle of a praying mantis only lasts for around one year. This means that after laying her eggs, the female praying mantis dies as winter comes back around.

Both the male and female may be dead, but the eggs laid in the ootheca keep the praying mantis life cycle going.

A GROSS LIFE

Praying mantises do other gross things. Some praying mantises can catch and eat small birds. When they do, they eat the birds' brains! Yuck!

Praying mantises are the only insects that can turn their heads around far enough to see behind them. That means you can't sneak up on a praying mantis!

How many ears do you have? Well, praying mantises only have one! It is on the bottom of their tummy. This means they cannot work out which **direction** noises come from.

Praying mantises are the only insect to have just one ear.

Some praying mantises are very good at hiding. Many hide so that their helpless prey won't notice them before they **pounce**.

GROSS LIFE CYCLE OF A PRAYING MANTIS

1. A female praying mantis lays eggs.

2. The female dies before winter.

3. Nymphs hatch and eat each other.

4. Adult mantises mate and the female may eat the male.

GET EXPLORING!

Have you ever seen a praying mantis? Some zoos have insect houses where you can see them up close and learn more about them.

GLOSSARY

direction The way something is coming from or moving toward.

hatch To come out of an egg.

insect An animal with one or two pairs of wings, six legs, and no backbone.

invisible Something you cannot see.

pounce To suddenly jump toward and take hold of something.

praying (In religion) Thanking, asking, or speaking to a god or some other spiritual being.

prey Animals that are hunted by other animals for food.

protects Stops something from coming to harm.

INDEX

adults 4, 8, 12, 22
brains 18
ears 20
eating 11, 15, 18, 22
eggs 8–10, 15–17, 22
heads 14–15, 19
hiding 21
insects 6, 19, 23
mating 12–15, 22
nymphs 10, 23
ootheca 9–10, 17
prey 6, 21

PHOTO CREDITS Images are courtesy of Shutterstock.com. With thanks to Getty Images, Thinkstock Photo, and iStockphoto.

Recurring images – Milan M (grunge shapes), Sonechko57 (splat shapes), Jojje, Infinity32829 (paper background), Rimma Z (watercolour splatters), Sopelkin, Wondervendy (decorative vectors). Cover – Eric Isslee, hchjjl, p2–3 –xpixel, Eric Isslee, Seregraff, p4–5 – Anatoly Tiplyashin, Here, maxim ibragimov, Djomas, p6–7 – Paul Looyen, BBA Photograph, p8–9 – Bankim Desa, Ryan M. Bolton, p10–11 – Evgeniy Ayupov, Amelia Martin, p12–13 – Ndanko, p14–15 – eleonimages, Warren Parker, p16–17 – eleonimages, GlanceDay, p18–19 – muhamad miza bin ngateni, In The Light Photography, p20–21 – oger Meerts, Melinda Fawver, p22–23 – Purino, Amelia Martin, Bayoeajie, LensMT, V.Lawren